AF610848

TRIET!

NOT DIET

LIFE CHANGING TRIET MENUS & HEALTH REMINDERS

TONY COLEMAN

Order this book online at www.trafford.com/07-1993
or email orders@trafford.com

Most Trafford titles are also available at major online book retailers.

© Copyright 2008 Tony Coleman.
Edited by Dan Smith
Cover Design/Artwork by Shani Goss
Photography by Christine Doolen

All rights reserved. No part of this publication may be reproduced, stored in a retrieval system, or transmitted, in any form or by any means, electronic, mechanical, photocopying, recording, or otherwise, without the written prior permission of the author.

Unless otherwise indicated, all Scripture quotations are taken from the
King James Version of the Bible

Note for Librarians: A cataloguing record for this book is available from Library and Archives Canada at www.collectionscanada.ca/amicus/index-e.html

ISBN: 978-1-4251-4657-3

We at Trafford believe that it is the responsibility of us all, as both individuals and corporations, to make choices that are environmentally and socially sound. You, in turn, are supporting this responsible conduct each time you purchase a Trafford book, or make use of our publishing services. To find out how you are helping, please visit www.trafford.com/responsiblepublishing.html

Our mission is to efficiently provide the world's finest, most comprehensive book publishing service, enabling every author to experience success. To find out how to publish your book, your way, and have it available worldwide, visit us online at www.trafford.com/10510

www.trafford.com

North America & international
toll-free: 1 888 232 4444 (USA & Canada)
phone: 250 383 6864 ♦ fax: 250 383 6804
email: info@trafford.com

The United Kingdom & Europe
phone: +44 (0)1865 722 113 ♦ local rate: 0845 230 9601
facsimile: +44 (0)1865 722 868 ♦ email: info.uk@trafford.com

10 9 8 7 6 5 4 3

I love you, Princess.

Acknowledgements

Thanks to God who gave me the credible idea to write this book and also all the advice and help from my friends and my family; especially my wife René for her support and understanding. The inspiration for this book comes from my son, Tyler, and the illness he endured as an infant prior to the lifestyle change that came with healthy eating.

"Beloved, I wish above all
things that thou mayest
prosper and be in health,
even as thy soul prospereth."

3 John 2

Tony's Triet menus are very easy to make. The food in the Triet are natural foods, including fresh fruits and raw nuts. Vegetables should be steamed when prepared and not cooked in boiling water. If you prepare the menus as they appear in this book, you will loose weight the natural way. You will also fuel your body with healthy foods that will heal the body.

It's God's plan for us to live a long healthy life, to prosper, and to live it abundantly. When we eat the wrong foods we are making room for diseases and other health problems to arise. The food that we choose to eat determines our health in the future.

Remember; Eat to Live, Not Die!

Moderate exercise must be apart of your "Triet Not Diet Plan".

If you don't have access to a local gym, there's always something you can do in your home.

- SIT UPS
- PUSH UPS
- WALK STAIRS
- RUN IN PLACE (1 minute, 5 reps)

Organic Echinacea Plus Tea is one of the best teas for building your immune system. You can find this all natural immune builder at your local health nutrition store.

In order for you to get the proper amount of daily water intake, divide your weight by two and that will give you the number of ounces of water you should drink daily.

Your choice of water should be bottled water, never tap water.

Eliminate soda pop completely from your diet.

Drink water daily!

TRIET MENU

Tony's Blueberry Salad Triet

Greenleaf lettuce (*iceberg lettuce holds no nutritional value*) mixed with green peppers, red peppers, cucumber, tomatoes, walnuts, & blueberries.

You can eat it plain or add olive oil (cold processed) as your dressing.

Tony's Energy Drink and Internal Cleanse Triet

Two tablespoons organic apple cider vinegar mixed with 8 oz. glass of distilled water. You can take three times a day, morning afternoon, & evening or anytime you need a pick-me-up.

This all natural drink also works as a body cleanse.

Eat to Survive, Not to get full!

TRIET MENU

Tony's Triet Dinner

Greenleaf lettuce salad with green peppers, red peppers, cucumber, walnuts, feta or other non-dairy cheese.
Eat plain or add cold processed olive oil.

Wild pacific salmon either baked or fried in olive oil or canola oil, season with organic seasoning of your choice & sea salt.

Baked sweet potato with honey and a tablespoon or two of olive oil.
(do not microwave, bake in oven)

"Tony's Triet Fruit Medley" for Dessert

1c. plain yogurt
Half cup organic blueberries
Fresh sliced oranges
Half cup walnuts
Add honey

TRIET MENU

"Tony's Triet Breakfast"

Whole grain oatmeal or cereal with rice milk or soy milk, add honey or Stevia.
(Stevia is a natural sweetener)

Whole grain toast with flaxseed & fresh fruit of your choice. Use olive oil to spread on your toast in place of butter or margarine.
Organic blueberry or strawberry jelly in place of regular jelly.

Turkey sausage, turkey bacon if you desire
(Organic and Free Range)
(*eat in moderation*)

Organic apple juice or bottled water (*filtered*)

Always keep in mind breakfast and lunch should be your largest meal.

"TRIET"

TRIET MENU

"TONY'S TRIET LUNCH"

Greenleaf lettuce salad with tomatoes, green peppers, red peppers, cucumber, walnuts, almonds, organic cheese.
Use olive oil (cold processed)

Grilled or baked, fried tilapia in olive oil, chicken breast (*free range*). You can add this to your salad or eat it separately.

Bottled water (*filtered*) with lemon

Tony's Triet Menu's will fill you up as well as keep you HEALTHY.

TRIET MENU

Tony's Triet Snacks

Almonds, walnuts, carrots, apples, veggie chips, (*great for afternoon Triet*).

Plain yogurt with fresh fruit of your choice sliced in small pieces.

Extra dark chocolate candy bar with cranberries and macadamia nuts are a great source of fiber. You can find these delicious bars at any health nutrition store. (*eat in moderation*).

Organic peanut butter and blueberry sandwich. (*whole grain bread*).

Rice milk or soy milk as your Triet drink of choice.

Triet Menu

Tony's Triet Mix

Whole grain Cheerios, Whole grain Chex, almonds, walnuts, dried organic apples, apricots, pine apples, blueberries, and sunflower seeds.

Triet Menu

Tony's Fruit Mix

Plain yogurt, add blueberries, apples, fresh fruit, walnuts, almonds & a drizzle of honey.

This makes for a great snack.

TRI-LICIOUS!

Tony's Triet Reminder

If it's modified, pasteurized, hydrogenised, high fructose corn syrup, it can clog arteries.

Moderate exercise 3 days a week

If you don't have access to a gym use what you do have:

- Walk your stairs.
- Do sit ups or crunches.
- Jump Rope
- Push Ups
- Lift Weights
- Walk

"TRI- SOMETHING"

Tony's Triet Reminder

Try to be finished with your last meal around 6 pm or 7 pm.

Go for a 30 minute brisk walk after dinner. Don't sit in front of the television right after a meal.

Tony's Triet Menu's are designed to feed and fuel your body with natural and healthy foods that were meant for you to enjoy.
Tony's Triet Menu's are for you to slowly phase into your health style, until you are comfortable with eating and living healthy.

DON'T KNOCK IT UNTIL YOU "TRIET"

Triet Menu

Tony's Breakfast & Lunch

Oatmeal with two tablespoons of honey or Stevia.

Whole grain toast with flaxseed, use olive oil in place of butter or margarine. Use Organic blueberry or strawberry jelly.

Fresh fruit, apple, banana, peach, orange, papaya, any fresh fruit will do.

Tall glass of freshly juiced apple or orange juice. If you do not have a juicer, it's a must have.

Green leaf lettuce salad with walnuts, green peppers, red peppers, black olives, cucumbers, organic cheese, add olive oil as your dressing.

Baked Salmon, Steamed Veggies.

Triet Menu

Tony's Triet Dinner Menu

Green leaf lettuce salad of course with all the fixn's. Green peppers, red peppers, blueberries, cucumber, walnuts, tomatoes, organic cheese.
Olive oil & apple cider vinegar

Baked or regular sweet potato, add a couple of tablespoons of honey to give it a little Triet flavor.

Tony's Triet Reminder

Breakfast and lunch should always be your largest meals. Try swapping breakfast and lunch around once a week to shake things up.

"TRIET"

Tony's Triet Reminder

The food that we eat determines the way our bodies operate.

For example, if you go out and by a brand new car (*Midnight Blue Corvette*), you're going to do all you can to keep that car performing at it's best (*RIGHT*). Top grade fuel, oil, & tires. So, why should we treat our bodies any differently?

We can always go out and buy another car; we can't go out and buy another body.

God made our bodies to perform at their very best, always, even as we get older; not just some of the time.

Healthy eating is the way to keep our bodies in top shape, always. Again, what we put in our amazing bodies will determine how our bodies will perform. Why not treat our bodies like a brand new car all the time!

Tony's Triet Dessert Menu

Fresh Fruit Triet: Apples, oranges, pineapple, strawberries, blueberries, papaya, & walnuts, Add plain yogurt if you so desire. (*do not add sugar*)
Drizzle honey over top.

Tony's Smoothy Triet: Crushed ice, bananas, blueberries, strawberries, kiwi, and low-fat whip topping. Add honey to taste.

Tony's baked Walnut Apple Triet: Baked walnuts & sliced apples (*thin sliced*)
Shower with cinnamon
Place in oven at 350 for 10 to 15 minutes
Remove from oven & drizzle honey all over.
Let cool.

Remember, there are all kinds of all natural desserts that are healthy that you can put together yourself. You have to be creative.

TRI-MENDOUS!

Triet Menu

Tony's Triet Breakfast

Whole grain cereal with either rice milk, almond milk, or soy milk.

Two scrambled eggs (*free range*)

Free range means poultry are allowed to roam free to get exercise, eat, and grow naturally with no human interference.

Whole grain toast, whole grain English muffin, or bagel. Add organic strawberry or blueberry jelly.

Sliced apples or oranges.

Tall glass of freshly juiced fruit of your liking.

Tony's Triet Lunch

Green Leaf lettuce salad with cucumbers, tomatoes, black olives, green peppers, red peppers, walnuts.
Use olive oil as your dressing.

Baked or grilled chicken breast sandwich on whole grain bread.
You can prepare the chicken breast the night before.
Add slices of tomato and non-dairy cheese.

Bottled water (*filtered*) with a slice of lemon.

Have an apple for your dessert or plain yogurt.

Remember; eat to survive,

not to get full!

Triet Menu

Tony's Triet Dinner

Green leaf lettuce or romaine salad, green peppers, red peppers, cucumber, black olives, walnuts, use olive oil as your salad dressing.

Baked salmon or tilapia. If you desire you may fry in olive or canola oil. A good indicator in knowing the salmon is done is when the skin breaks away freely, or with the tilapia, it will flake easily.
Whole grain bread & steamed vegetables.
(*try frying your fresh veggies in olive oil*)

This meal will not bc complete unless you have a glass of red wine to go with it. If you like, have a glass of bottled water (*filtered*) with a lemon slice. No tap water!

For dessert, try plain yogurt with organic apple slices or blueberries with honey drizzled over it.

Triet Menu

Tony's Triet Breakfast

Fresh organic apple slices, blueberries, strawberries, or pineapples, or the fresh fruit of your choice.

Slice of whole grain toast with organic blueberry or strawberry jelly.
Use olive oil in place of butter or margarine.

Tony's Triet Lunch

Brown rice with either red or black beans. There's a host of other beans that you may choose also.

Green leaf salad with cucumber, tomato, green peppers, red peppers, & walnuts.

Use olive oil with apple cider vinegar as your salad dressing.

Triet Menu

Tony's Organic Pizza Triet

Whole grain pizza crust
Tomato paste
Tomatoes, onion, mushrooms, green and red peppers, black olives
Feta & mozzarella cheese
Baked chicken breast cut in medium size pieces.

Heat oven 375 to 400 degrees, depending on the oven.

Bake until crust is golden brown.

Use sea salt to season (*in moderation*)

Small green leaf lettuce salad with all the fixn's cucumber, green and red peppers, walnuts, almonds, mushrooms. Apple Cider Vinegar as your salad dressing.

Glass of bottled water with lemon slice.

Triet Menu

Tony's Triet Breakfast

Small piece of fruit of your choice.

Bowl of whole grain cereal hot or cold add walnuts or almonds, blueberries, strawberries. Use honey in place of sugar or Stevia.

Tony's Triet Lunch

Green leaf salad, tomatoes, green and red peppers, feta cheese, & cucumbers.

Add salmon to salad if you have any left over from dinner.

Use olive oil and Balsamic vinegar for dressing.

Whole grain bagel or bread.

Glass of bottled water (*filtered*) with lemon.

Triet Menu

Tony's Triet Dinner

Tilapia baked or fried in olive oil or canola oil.
Brown rice. Baked, plain, or sweet potato. Add olive oil to potato in place of butter or margarine. Try drizzling a little honey or Stevia over your potato.

Tony's Triet Reminder

You cannot ever live the life of your choice without coming face to face with what you eat.

Eat responsible, free to live life the way God foreordained for us to live.

Take unhealthy foods out of your lifestyle, health style, and make better choices.

Eat smaller portions.

Add healthy foods as a way of life.

Make a decision. You deserve the best life possible. It's there for the taking! Go out and get it. T. R. I. E. T.

The best way to loose weight and stay healthy, is to reprogram your way of eating, not thinking.

Let's not think in terms of loosing weight, let's think in terms of eating healthy.

Living foods, whole grains, fresh, organic fruits & free range foods; if you start today eating these types of natural foods, you will lose weight the natural way with moderate exercise, and the weight will stay off forever.

Tony's Triet Menu's are delicious, healthy, and will get you back on the road to a healthy lifestyle.

Triet Menu

Tony's Triet Reminder

Educate yourself on reading what ingredients you should avoid when buying foods.

If you cannot pronounce it, don't buy it.

Listed below are a few ingredients to be aware of:

- Monosodium Glutamate: MSG, physical problems.
- Aspartame: Physical problems, headaches, weight gain.
- High fructose corn syrup: Makes you fat.
- Hydrogenated Vegetables Oil: Trans Fat causes heart disease.
- Partially Hydrogenated Vegetable Oil: Trans fats & heart disease.
- Vegetable Oil, Corn Oil: Trans fats & clogged arteries.
- Sugar: very addicting, numerous health problems, too many to mention.

- Splenda: Man made.
- Dextrose: Chemically made, not natural, another name for sugar.
- Enriched: Bleached or white flour.
- Artificial Color: Man made

And that's just to name a few. There are countless more to lookout for. There are so many things we eat that are very harmful to our bodies.

Again, let's reprogram our minds on what we choose to eat.

Let's eat healthy, Let's stay healthy, Let's live healthy.

Let's live the way God intended for us to live; a long prosperous life.

Tony's Triet Reminder

It's up to you to do a little or a lot based on what you feel good about. Even making some simple adjustments and changes to your eating habits could have a dramatic impact.

WATER, WATER, WATER

I cannot emphasize enough that water (*bottled & filtered*) is one of the best things we can consume for our health. Water helps aid in nearly every body function we have including circulation to all cells of the body. Water also helps in the removal of waste via the blood stream and excretory organs.

Adequate water intake also slows the aging process, helps in the prevention of headaches, improves blood pressure, and relieves arthritis, back pain, and neck pain.

Water is so vital to our everyday lives.

Tony's Banana Triet Surprise

Peel 3 to 4 bananas, cut into medium size chunks, place on small tray & put in freezer for about 2 to 3 hours.
Place frozen chunks in blender or food processor & beat until thick and creamy.
Add honey, walnuts or almonds.
You may serve this in a bowl or on an ice cream cone.

Tony's Fruit Syrup Triet

Add a cup or two of strawberries, 2 tbsp of balsamic vinegar, & 1 tbsp of Stevia to blender & mix until it becomes liquid.

Pour over whole grain pancakes, waffles, French toast, ice cream (*non-dairy*) or fresh fruit.

"TRI-LICIOUS"

Triet Menu

Tony's Apple Salad Triet

Chopped organic apples with green leaf lettuce, place in bowl and mix. Add green and red peppers, walnuts or almonds, lemon juice. Toss and add olive oil & balsamic vinegar as your salad dressing.

Tony's Healthy Salad Dressing Triet

4 Tablespoons of plain yogurt
2 Tablespoons of lemon juice
2 Tablespoons of olive oil (*extra virgin*)
Mix well. Try on baked or grilled salmon, tilapia, or chicken, and of course, salad.

Tony's Healthy Olive Oil and Balsamic Vinegar Dressing

2 Cups of Extra Virgin olive oil
2 Cups of Balsamic Vinegar
2 Tablespoons of sea salt
Mix together add to salad

Tony's Triet Reminder

Triet's Six Healthiest Foods

- Blackberries
- Walnuts
- Strawberries
- Artichoke Heart
- Cranberries
- Blueberries

These six foods have natural chemicals and antioxidants that help prevent diseases.

Remember eat lots of leafy green vegetables. It will help you lose weight, boost your heart health, and also fight against aging.

Limit salt as it contributes to weight retention.
Add fiber such as brown rice, whole grain bread, beans, & oatmeal. Fiber slows your digestion down so you won't over eat.

Tony's Triet Reminder

The basis for my Triet Menu's are raw fruits, raw vegetables, nuts, seeds, fish, free range meats (*in moderation*), exercise, & water.

In the beginning, God created man and told him what his diet should consist of. When we ignore God's design for how we should live and eat our bodies malfunction physically, emotionally, and mentally.

A person should eat three to five servings of vegetables a day and two to four servings of fruit daily. Just by adding this to your "Triet" you'll be amazed how much better you feel.

The more fresh fruit you eat the more you will find that most other desserts are too sweet to eat.

It's a TRIET, not a diet!

Triet Menu

Tony's Honey and Yogurt Triet

Half cup of honey added to a pint of plain yogurt.
May be heated slightly, or in the summer months the yogurt can be chilled.
Add walnuts or almonds to give you that extra crunch.

Tony's Triet Reminder

Keep healthy snacks around such as fruit, nuts, seeds, blueberries, strawberries, apples, or
carrots. Prior to going grocery shopping, eat a healthy snack. Doing so will keep you from buying unhealthy pastries.

Try not to eat for any reason other than to fuel the body.

Remember the brand new car theory. The fuel that we put in our bodies determines how the body will perform.

Triet Menu

Tony's Triet Reminder

The American diet is too high in red meats, salt, sugar, processed foods, & saturated fats.

The American diet lacks fresh fruit, vegetables and whole grains, seeds & nuts.

TRIET REMINDER

- Cook and bake with whole grain products, eat more fresh fruits and vegetables, beans, legumes, and nuts.

- Substitute olive oil for butter, margarine, & salad dressings. Avoid fried or deep fried foods.

- Limit your cheese intake to small amounts. Use feta cheese or parmesan. Do not eat block cheese.

- Choose fish (*wild fish, not farmed raised*) and poultry (*free range poultry*) over red meat.

Tony's Live Foods and Health Style

Triet Makeover

Meat: Free range (*in moderation*)
Milk: Skim milk, rice milk, almond milk, plain yogurt, cottage cheese
Nuts: Walnuts, almonds (*keep nuts in sealed bag after opening and store in refrigerator*)
Olive Oil: Extra virgin olive oil (*cold processed*)
Starches: Brown rice, wild rice, legumes, beans, potatoes (*fresh*)
Sweets: Honey, Stevia
Vegetables: Fresh or frozen broccoli, carrots, peppers, olives, spinach, collard greens, tomatoes, green leaf or romaine lettuce (*iceberg lettuce holds no nutritional value*), cauliflower, & asparagus
Vinegar: Balsamic, Apple
Wine: 4–8 oz. glass of red wine with dinner (*holds the most health value over white wines*)
Fish: Wild salmon, tilapia (*choose fish with scales*)

Triet Menu
Tony's Dining Out Triet Reminder

When ordering your salad, choose your dressing on the side, & choose vinegar and oil. If possible, always choose green leaf lettuce as iceberg lettuce holds no nutritional value.

You can split your entrée of fish, poultry, meat (*sparingly*), steamed vegetables, sweet or plain baked potato.

Politely tell your waitress to ask the chef if they will use olive oil in place of butter.

Vegetable base soups are healthier than cream based soups.

Request whole grain breads & bottled water with a lemon slice for your drink.

Triet Menu

Tony's Avocado and Celery Salad

Triet

2 tbsp. extra virgin olive oil
2 tbsp. organic mayonnaise
1 tbsp. hot mustard juice & add 1 lemon juice
2 c. celery, chopped in ½ inch pieces
1c. chopped sweet white onions
1c. of diced red peppers
1c. of diced green peppers
1 large ripe avocado peeled and chopped in ½ inch pieces

In large bowl combine olive oil, organic mayonnaise, mustard lemon juice, and sea salt to taste and whisk.

Add celery, onion, and bell pepper. Mix well. Add the avocado & gently toss.

Triet Menu

Tony's Broccoli Medley Triet

1 tbsp. extra virgin olive oil
1 clove of garlic minced
1 ¼ lb. of broccoli cut into bite sizes
½ red and green peppers cut into strips
½ yellow pepper cut into strips
2 tbsp. organic soy sauce

Heat olive oil and garlic in skillet or wok

Add broccoli and stir fry for 1 minute

Add peppers and continue to stir fry for 3 to 4 minutes more or until vegetables are crisp. Add soy sauce, cook and stir until heated through.

DON'T KNOCK IT UNTIL YOU "TRIET"

Triet Menu

Tony's Honey Glazed Carrots

1 lb. Medium carrots, peeled or 1 lb. baby carrots
2 tbsp. filtered bottled water
1 tbsp. pure honey
1 tsp. extra virgin olive oil
¼ tsp. nutmeg

Cut medium carrots in half lengthwise into 2 inch pieces or cut baby carrots in half lengthwise. In a large skillet cook carrots covered, in a small amount of boiling water for 8 minutes until tender. Drain.

Add 2 tbsp water, honey, olive oil, and nutmeg to skillet. Stir, bring to a boil, and cook about 2 minutes more. Stir often until carrots are glazed. Season with sea salt & serve.

Triet Menu

Tony's Pecan and String Beans

Triet

1 lb. fresh string beans
1 medium sliced onion
1 tbsp. olive oil
Add salt (*sea salt*) organic pepper to taste
½ cup of pecan halves

Place olive oil in a skillet on medium heat. Add string beans and then pecans stirring frequently for 15 minutes. Serve.

Tony's Reminder

Know the limits on fat and salt intake as well as sugar. Look for foods low in saturated fats and zero trans fats. Choose and prepare foods and beverages with limited amounts of salts, sugars, & high fructose corn syrup.

Tony's Triet Reminder

Eat more Fresh Organic Fruits and "Vegetables"

Remember we are truly what we eat. Eating fresh fruit and vegetables can lead to healthier, firmer skin. Fresh fruit provides vitamins and is a key for healthy looking skin. Blueberries are also great for the skin and immune system.
Lemons can be used on the skin to exfoliate.

Eating fresh steamed vegetables gives the skin vitamins and minerals to stay free of skin break-outs.

Omega 3 fatty acids found in salmon, sardines, & walnuts help reducc skin inflammation and increase blood circulation which fights wrinkles. (*Natural Face Lift*)

Tony's Feta Cheese and Spinach Dip

Triet

1 8 oz. carton of plain yogurt
¾ cup crumbled feta cheese
2 oz. low fat cream cheese, softened
¼ cup low-fat sour cream
1 garlic clove, crushed
1 ½ cup finely chopped spinach
1 tbsp minced fresh dried dill
⅛ tsp black pepper

Spoon yogurt onto several layers of wax paper no more than ½" thickness.
Cover with additional wax paper and let stand 5 minutes.

Scrape into bowl or food processor using rubber spatula. Add the cheeses, sour cream, garlic & process until smooth.

Spoon yogurt mixture into the bowl & stir in spinach, minced dill, & pepper and cover & chill for 10 to 15 minutes. Serve.

Triet Menu
Tony's Triet Reminder

When choosing organic fruit or vegetables, check the sticker that's affixed to the item.

If the number begins with a number 9, followed by four numbers, then it's truly organic.

If the number begins with a number 8, followed by four numbers, its not organic. It's been genetically modified or prematurely grown in someway.

If the number begins with a number 4, followed by three numbers, they have been sprayed with pesticides and other chemicals.

MY ADVICE TO YOU WOULD BE:
ALWAYS CHOOSE ORGANIC

Tony's Triet Reminder

Daily water Intake

We have all been told we must drink 8 8oz. glasses of water daily in order to get the proper amount of water intake and for our bodies to function to its full capacity.

NOT TRUE!

First of all, do not drink tap water. Why? Because it contains chlorine, fluoride, and a host of other bacteria that may cause health problems. Remember the tap water that we drink is also used for, bathing, washing clothes, and toilet water (*not good*).

In order to find out how much water one should drink on a daily basis, take your body weight and divide that by two. This formula will give you the total number of ounces you should drink daily.

Tony's All Natural Triet Dinner

Large green leaf lettuce salad with your choice of fresh vegetables. Olive oil & apple cider vinegar as your dressing.

Brown rice, baked or grilled chicken breast. Baked sweet potato with a tablespoon of honey.

Whole grain bread of your choice.
(*no butter or margarine*)

Bottled water with Lemon slice.
(*not tap water*)

Snack Yogurt (*plain*) with walnuts and/or blueberries & two tablespoons of honey.

Triet Menu

Tony's Seed's And Nuts Triet

Walnuts, Almonds, Sunflower Seeds, Pumpkin Seeds, (*unsalted*) Macadamia Nuts, Pistachio's.

Remember these nuts and seeds should not be roasted or salted. Enjoy them in moderation.

Tony's Triet Reminder

The living nutrients found in raw foods as well as their juices is what satisfies our nutritional needs, helping with hunger cravings. Also, living foods provide for more energy and improved health.

Tony's Helpful Triet Hints

Asparagus is a wonderful source of folate, great for heart health.

Green Peas are a great source for B Vitamins including B1, B2, B3, B6 and Folate, which promotes healthy vision & contains powerful antioxidants.

Apricots are great for heart health as they reduce cholesterol.

Spinach contains carotenoids which are very important for cardiovascular & bone health, and also has cancer fighting properties.

Avocados contain monosaturated fats which help lower cholesterol. They also have more potassium than bananas.

Romaine & green leaf lettuce are great for the heart as they contain beta-carotene.

Tony's Protein Triet's

- Black Beans
- Kale
- Sunflower Seeds
- Alfalfa Sprouts
- Avocado

Tony's Calcium Triet's

- Almonds
- Green Beans
- Broccoli
- Carrot Juice

These are just a few of the protein and calcium living and raw foods that you can add to you "TRIET"

Tony's Triet Reminder

Choose a wide range of foods & eat plenty of fruits and vegetables.

Protein: keeps muscles, skin, teeth, and other tissue healthy. Most of us have no trouble getting enough protein. Lean meat, fish, poultry (*free range*), beans, eggs, and nuts are a good source of protein.

Carbohydrates: Eat plenty of fruits and vegetables. Also eat whole grains like brown rice, multigrain bread, and whole wheat pasta.

Fiber: Fiber rich foods help you feel more full, longer, which may help you loose weight. Fruit, vegetables, and whole grains are good sources of fiber.

Fats: No more than a third of your calories each day should come from fat.

Tony's "EX-TRI-CISE" Triet

You should get at least 30 minutes of moderate "EX-TRI-CISE" on most days of the week.

It's even better if you can be active everyday.

If 30 minutes is too much starting out, breakup your workouts into 10 minute periods throughout the day.

Start slowly & build up your "EX-TRI-CISE" over time.

Don't beat yourself up for slipups; instead, try to get back on target as soon as you can.

Keep a record of your progress; that will give you incentive to stay on your "EX-TRI-CISE" program.

YOU CAN DO IT! "TRIET"

Tony's Triet Reminder

"TRI-MAZING ALMONDS"

This nutritious nut appears to be even better for your heart than originally thought.

Adding almonds to your Triet can lower your total cholesterol, as well as your LDL bad cholesterol.

Almonds are high in Vitamin E, mono-unsaturated fat and fiber. Almonds may help reduce other risk factors for heart disease also.

Eat almonds to help promote heart health.

It's the small things we do that will help us live a long and healthy life.

"TRIET"

Tony's Triet Reminder

FRUIT – Simply TRIET

Keep a bowl of whole fruit in a visible spot, such as on the kitchen table, counter, or an eye level shelf.

Add crushed pineapple, diced apples, or sliced red grapes to plain yogurt or cottage cheese.

Make your own fruit kabobs; skewer bananas, berries, & pineapples chunks. This will make a great TRIET snack.

For dessert try baked apples, pears, or peaches drizzled with honey.

"TRI-LICIOUS"

Tony's Bell Pepper and Salsa Triet

Instead of the same old Tortilla Chips, dip fresh bell peppers slices in salsa.

Try Salsa as a salad dressing with green leaf lettuce and spinach salad.

Keep cut veggies in a clear container in your refrigerator for an easy & healthy Triet snack.

Always keep fresh vegetables on hand; you can never go wrong with these healthy and tasty treats!

Triet Did You Know

Fiber

Insoluble Fiber: coarse, chewy part of a plant that does not dissolve in water. It forms a plant's structure and can be found in the outside tissue.

Think fruit skins, stringy vegetables, and crunchy whole grains.

Its function includes passing through the body largely intact, soaking up water like a sponge & adding bulk and softness to the stool. This not only prevents constipation, but also speeds up the rate which foods go through your system.

Insoluble Fiber also moves harmful toxins and cancer causing substances in alcohol, pesticides, processed foods, preservatives and additives out of the colon.

Foods containing the most insoluble fiber:

- whole grain breads
- wheat bran
- rye
- cabbage
- beets
- carrots
- Brussels sprouts
- Turnips
- cauliflower
- apple skins

Soluble Fiber: found inside plant cell walls, dissolves and thickens in water to form a sticky, gel-like substance. It gives oatmeal its gummy texture and cooked beans their mushy center.

Its function includes passing through the digestive system & binding the dietary cholesterol helping the body to eliminate it. This reduces blood cholesterol levels, which may help reduce heart disease.

Foods containing the most soluble fiber:

- Oats
- Oat bran
- Beans
- Peas
- Rice bran
- Citrus fruit
- Strawberries
- Apple pulp

Fiber and water DO mix

Adding a lot of fiber to your Triet too quickly can cause gas, bloating and cramping. Increase fiber gradually over a period of a few weeks. Remember to drink plenty of water, which helps fiber pass smoothly through the digestive system.

Always eat whole grain; if the label doesn't say "100%," don't buy it. Check the ingredients for refined or misleading statements. Check for bleached or unbleached wheat flour & rice flour. If it contains any of these ingredients, it's not 100% whole grain.

Try other 100% whole grain foods such as brown rice, oatmeal, barley, & cracked wheat.

God Gave Man a Triet

The Bible goes on to say after God created man:

"God placed man in a garden, that garden was called the Garden Of Eden. He gave man his first ever diet."

And God said, "Behold, I have given you every herb bearing seed, which is upon the face of all the earth, and every tree, in the which is the fruit of a tree yielding seed; to you it shall be for meat." (Genesis 1:29)

"And to every beast of the earth, and to every fowl of the air, and to everything that creepeth upon the earth, wherein there is life, I have given every green herb for meat: and it was so." (Genesis 1:30)

Be aware how products are advertised; Natural does not necessarily mean organic. Organic means that no chemicals were used in growing and processing the food.

Always wash produce with tap water to remove the surface contaminants. You can also peel fruits and vegetables that are coated with wax.

Having knowledge of what you're putting in your body can prolong your life.

Tony's Triet Reminder

FISH

According to the Law of Moses, fish with scales and fins were clean (*edible*).

And those without were unclean, such as shell fish & catfish.

Numbers 11:5
"We remember the fish, which we did eat in Egypt freely; the cucumbers, and the melons, onions, and garlic"

Remember, these are also the foods that Jesus ate; all natural foods without the artificial additives and other health harming ingredients, are the foods Jesus intended for us to enjoy.

Fish should be consumed as often as possible. Salmon, tilapia, cod, & trout have amazing health benefits, considering the intake of Omega 3 from eating fish.

Omega 3 lowers cholesterol and helps rid and fight LDL, which is bad cholesterol. Eating fish is one of the most important health foods in the "TRIET".

Fish should be consumed 3 to 4 times a week & cooked in olive oil or canola oil & baked or grilled.

Leviticus 11:9-10

These shall ye eat of all that are in the waters: whatsoever hath fins and scales in the waters, in the seas, and in the rivers, them shall ye eat.

And all that have not fins and scales in the seas, and in the rivers, of all that move in the waters, and of any living thing which is in the waters, they shall be an abomination unto you.

"Remember; eat to live, not to die"

"TRIET"

Tony's Flax Seed Reminder

Flax Seed: Brown and Golden, whole as well as ground.

Flax seed is rich in Omega 3 and Omega 6 fatty acids, which have been shown to help lower cholesterol and work with fiber to promote heart health.

Buckwheat has been shown to regulate blood pressure and lower cholesterol.

Mixed grain cereals add a variety of grains to your Triet which gives the body extra fiber and helps regulate blood cholesterol.

Bran also adds fiber which gives you the feeling of being full and binds to cholesterol to help eliminate it from the body.

"MOST IMPORTANT"

TRIET REMINDER

It's difficult to gain weight eating only natural foods!

Eat plenty of:

- *Fresh, Organic Vegetables*
- *Fresh, Organic Fruits*
- *Whole Grain Foods*
- *Nuts, Walnuts, Almonds, Pistachios*
- *Plain Yogurts*
- *Fish, especially salmon, tilapia & other fish with scales as they protect the fish from bacteria and other chemicals from entering the fish*

Tony's Sugar Cleanse Triet

Eat plenty of vegetables, and fruit, especially pears, apples, citrus, & berries. These are a must as they are full of vitamins and healthy antioxidants.

Eat lean protein soy, fish, beans, and chicken. Remember, protein helps keep blood sugar stable.

Consume healthy fats in moderation such as olive oil, flaxseed oil, and nuts. These fats help keep your hunger in check.

Try to avoid foods such as corn, potatoes, beets, mangoes, dates, bananas, watermelons, grapes, raisins. These foods can create instability in blood sugar levels, causing mood swings and cravings.

Also avoid sugar, white flour, regular pasta, & dairy.

Five Healing Taste Triets

Sweet: apples, apricots, cherries, dates, figs, beets, carrots, sweet potatoes, squash, coconuts, & sesame seeds. Also, honey helps energize, relax dry cough, and calms you.

Sour: rye, green peppers, zucchini, lemons, limes, pickles, & vinegar helps with diarrhea, urinary problems, & hemorrhoids.

Bitter: alfalfa, romaine lettuce, sunflower seeds, helps inflammation, infections, constipation, and swelling.

Salty: buckwheat, black beans, kale, mushrooms, water chestnuts, & unrefined table salt helps muscles, cataracts, sore throat, & constipation.

Pungent: ginger, garlic, hot peppers, onions, asparagus, & broccoli aids in digestion.

When you balance the five tastes' to your daily Triet you can improve immune function, health, and a host of other health related matters.

Why Iron?

It carries oxygen in red blood cells to your tissues, supplying energy.

Eat more vegetables along with vitamin C

Why Calcium?

Essential for strong teeth, and bones.

Decrease your salt intake

Why Vitamin D?

May have cancer fighting qualities, promotes healthy teeth and bones. Good sources include salmon, mackerel, and cod liver oil.

Why Folate Acid?

Lowers heart disease. "Fortifies cereals"

Tony's Ginger, Pear, and Honey Triet Sauce

4 ripe pears peeled, remove core & cut into ½ inch chunks
2-3 tsp fresh lemon juice
2 tbsp almond oil or canola oil
1 tsp ground cinnamon
1 pinch ground all spice
3 tablespoons honey
½ teaspoon vanilla extract
¼ cup finely chopped crystallized ginger
1/3 cup finely chopped pecans, toasted

Combined pears and lemon juice in a mixing bowl and toss to combine.

Heat oil in large skillet over medium heat. Add pears and cook. Stir occasionally, until golden brown, 3-5 min. Reduce heat (*medium*) & add cinnamon and all spice, toss to combine. Add honey and cook. Stir occasionally, until pears are soft and juices syrupy, 2-3 min.

Remove from heat, stir in vanilla, ginger, and pecans. Serve immediately.

Use with Pancakes (*whole grain*) French toast, plain yogurt.

"TRI-LICIOUS"

Tony's Salmon Salad Triet with Blackberries, Walnuts, and Honey

1 lb Salmon Fillet
3 tbsp olive oil
¼ c. grape fruit juice
4 c. mixed salad greens
1 c. blackberries
½ c. chopped walnuts toasted
1 tbsp honey

Wash salmon & pat dry, heat 1 tbsp of olive oil in medium skillet. Cook salmon skin side for 1 min. Turn over & sprinkle with sea salt. Add garlic, cover & cook 10 min. or until cooked through.

While salmon is cooking, combine remaining 2 tbsp of olive oil, grapefruit juice, & honey in a small bowl, whisk well. Combine salad greens, toss, add vinegar and oil to salad. Place salad on plate, place salmon in middle sprinkle with walnuts and drizzle with more dressing. Add blackberries as desired.

"Tony's Miracle Food's that Heal"

Apples: Protects heart

Apricots: Controls blood pressure

Artichokes: Lowers cholesterol & smoothes skin

Avocados: Lowers cholesterol & blood pressure, battles diabetes

Bananas: Strengthens bones

Beans: Stabilizes sugar & lowers cholesterol

Beets: Protects your heart & aids in weight loss

Blueberries: Boosts memory & prevents constipation

Broccoli: Helps eyesight & lowers blood pressure

Cabbage: Promotes weight loss & prevents constipation

Cantaloupe: Supports immune system

Carrots: Protects eyesight & promotes weight loss

Cauliflower: Strengthens bones, guards against heart disease

Cherries: Slows aging process & protects heart

Chili peppers: Boosts immune system

Fish: Protects the heart, boosts memory & supports immune system

Flax: Aids digestion & boosts immune system

Garlic: Lowers cholesterol & controls blood pressure

Grapefruit: Promotes weight loss & lowers cholesterol

Grapes: Enhances blood flow, prevents kidney stones

Green Tea: Promotes weight loss

Honey: Fights allergies & increases energy

Lemons: Smoothes skin

Limes: Smoothes skin & controls blood pressure

Mangoes: Aids digestion

Mushrooms: Strengthens bones

Olive Oil: Smoothes skin, promotes weight loss & battles diabetes

Onions: Lowers cholesterol

Oranges: Supports immune system

Peaches: Aids digestion & prevents constipation

Peanuts: Promotes weight loss & lowers cholesterol

Pineapple: Strengthens bones & relieves colds

Prunes: Slows aging process & boosts memory

Brown Rice: Protects heart; helps with diabetes

Strawberries: Boosts memory & calms stress

Sweet Potatoes: Helps eyesight & strengthens bones

Tomatoes: Protects prostate & lowers cholesterol

Walnuts: Lowers cholesterol, protects against heart disease

Water: Promotes weight loss, smoothes skin & and a host of other cures

Watermelon: Controls blood pressure & lowers cholesterol

Wheat bran: Improves Digestion

Yogurt: Supports Immune System

Tony's Triet Reminder

Deuteronomy 8:8

"A land of wheat, and barley, and vines, and fig trees, and pomegranates; a land of oil olive, and honey…"

3 John 2

"Beloved, I wish above all things that thou mayest prosper and be in health, even as thy soul prospereth."

Again, I can't say this enough that it was, and still is God's will for us as human beings, to be in good health and eat the foods he created for us to eat. Sickness and disease were never part of God's plan for our physical bodies.

Thank you for taking time out of your busy schedule to choose a long and healthy life and to read

Triet, Not Diet Life Changing Triet Menus & Health Reminders

It is recommended that you always consult your physician before starting any type of diet or exercise program.

www.ingramcontent.com/pod-product-compliance
Ingram Content Group UK Ltd.
Pitfield, Milton Keynes, MK11 3LW, UK
UKHW020136250726
13967UKWH00002B/682

9 781425 146573